PROJECT WILDLIFE

TIGER

Michael Bright

DISCARD

Gloucester Press

New York : London : Toronto : Sydney

Introduction

The tiger is the largest and most powerful of the big cats. It has always held a special fascination for people. It has also attracted the attention of hunters, both for sport and for trade. Rows of mounted tiger heads decorate hunters' trophy rooms. They are a sad and permanent reminder of people's determination to destroy wild and dangerous animals. And thousands of tigers have been shot for their beautifully patterned skins. Tiger skin rugs and fur coats used to be very popular and people were prepared to pay a lot of money for them.

In recent years, the tiger has also been losing its living space to farming. As populations increase, more and more land is needed to feed people. This combination of hunting and loss of habitat had a serious effect on the tiger. It was brought to the brink of extinction. But then the tiger became the focus of international concern and Project Tiger was launched. The disaster was turned into a conservation success story. The tiger has been saved.

TIGER

CONTENTS

Introduction	4
Tiger distribution	7

The decline of the tiger

Hunters of the past	8
Hunting today	11
The tiger trade	12
Habitat destruction	14

Saving the tiger

Project Tiger	16
Reserves and research	18
Man-eating tigers	20
Tigers in zoos	23
The future of the tiger	24

Tiger fact files	26-31
Index	32

© Aladdin Books Ltd 1988

Designed and produced by
Aladdin Books Ltd
70 Old Compton Street
London W1

Design Rob Hillier
Editor Denny Robson
Researcher Cecilia Weston-Baker
Illustrator Ron Hayward Associates

*First published in the
United States in 1989 by*
Gloucester Press
387 Park Avenue South
New York, NY 10016

ISBN 0-531-17141-8

Library of Congress Catalog
Card Number: 88-83105

Printed in Belgium

▽ The tiger is a solitary and almost invisible animal in its natural habitat.

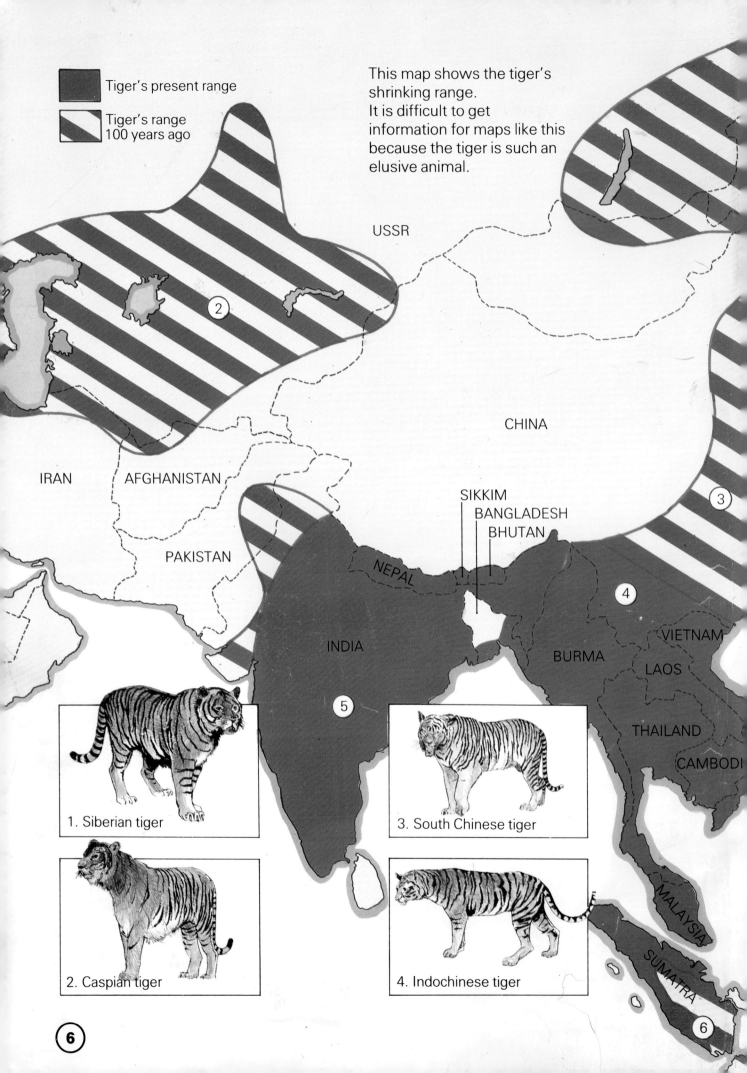

Tiger's present range

Tiger's range 100 years ago

This map shows the tiger's shrinking range.
It is difficult to get information for maps like this because the tiger is such an elusive animal.

USSR

CHINA

IRAN

AFGHANISTAN

PAKISTAN

NEPAL

SIKKIM
BANGLADESH
BHUTAN

INDIA

BURMA

VIETNAM

LAOS

THAILAND

CAMBODI

MALAYSIA

SUMATRA

1. Siberian tiger

2. Caspian tiger

3. South Chinese tiger

4. Indochinese tiger

Tiger distribution

There were once eight different types of tiger distributed throughout Asia. They lived in a variety of widely differing places, from tropical rain forest to snow-covered coniferous forest, and from dry grassland to mangrove swamps.

The largest tiger, the Siberian or Manchurian, still lives in the eastern Siberian forests and in northern China and Korea. There are no more than 300 left in the wild. The Indian or Bengal tiger is the most numerous, with over 3,000 remaining. It is found in isolated patches across India. The Indochinese or Corbett's tiger is found in Southeast Asia. Its numbers were considerably reduced during the Vietnam War. The South Chinese tiger has been considered an agricultural pest and it is doubtful if many are alive today. The Caspian tiger is barely surviving in western Asia. A few are thought to live in the mountains of northern Iran and Afghanistan. A few hundred Sumatran tigers are left, but only three or four Javan tigers remain. It is unlikely that the small population will survive. The smallest tiger, the Balinese, is extinct.

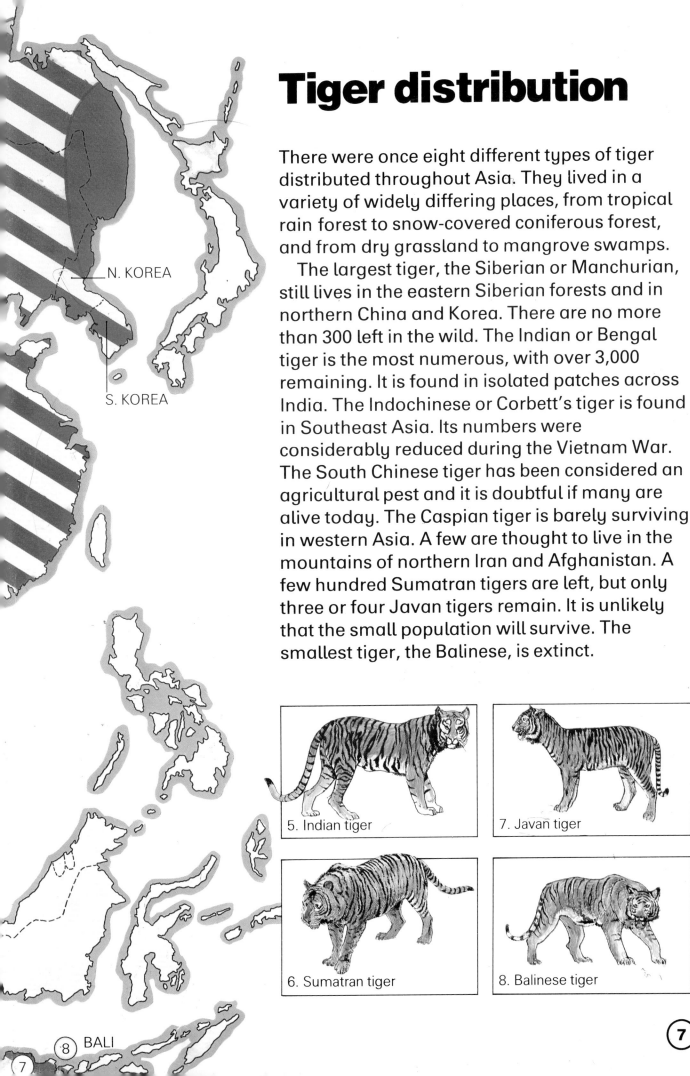

N. KOREA

S. KOREA

8 BALI

5. Indian tiger

7. Javan tiger

6. Sumatran tiger

8. Balinese tiger

Hunters of the past

In India, at the time of the British Empire in the 19th century, it was considered fashionable for army officers and government officials to "bag" a tiger. These hunters sat safely on the backs of elephants, while local "beaters" drove the animals towards the guns. A local marksman sat behind any important visitor who did not aim well. He shot at the approaching tiger at the same time as the guest, and the guest would think that he himself had shot the beast.

The Maharajah of Surguja claimed proudly that he had shot 1,157 tigers during his lifetime. The Maharajah of Scindia bagged 700 and his guests a further 200. Bengal Civil Servant George Yule stopped counting on his 400th.

This sport of the British Raj continued a tradition set by the Maharajahs, the rulers of India, who slaughtered tigers in their thousands. To kill a tiger was a status symbol. Long before there was talk of destruction of the tiger's habitat, the animal itself was being rapidly exterminated. At the beginning of the 20th century the tiger population in India was estimated at 40,000. A census in 1972 revealed that there were only 1,800 tigers left.

▽ The unfortunate animal in the photograph below is a Balinese tiger killed in 1925. No one will ever see one of these animals alive again. The last one was seen in 1952.

"In parts of India at the beginning of last century, tigers were so numerous it seemed to be a question as to whether man or tiger would survive."

A.A. Dunbar Brander, British Indian Forest Service (1927)

Hunting today

▷ This tiger head is a hunter's trophy.

This tigress is caught in a trap, like the one seen on the left. It snaps shut when a paw is put on the central trigger.

In most countries where tigers live in the wild it is against the law to kill them. Nevertheless, poaching and unofficial hunting is common. In India and Nepal, tiger hunting has been banned since 1972, yet today tigers are still killed. They are mainly poisoned. Local poachers lace carcasses of domestic animals with poison, usually highly toxic pesticides. The tigers find these easy meals and are killed.

In Sumatra, despite legal protection, the tiger is still hunted — sometimes by local officials who ignore the law. Leghold traps are put down at watering places and along deer trails. The tiger is caught and may remain there in agony for two days before the poacher returns. It is then killed with a spear.

Wherever there is conflict between the interests of tigers and farmers, such as in China, tigers are killed illegally. In some of these places, tigers are not killed immediately but are taken alive. Later they are butchered and eaten by the community.

The tiger trade

Tigers are killed illegally for their skins and their meat. The rewards are so high and the local people are so poor, it is a great temptation to become a poacher. A peasant may earn only $30 a year, yet he can sell a tiger skin for $3,000. The skins are traded via Hong Kong, Singapore and Bangkok and a tiger skin coat in Japan can be sold for $50,000.

Tiger meat is also valuable. In Taiwan, people believe that it keeps them warm in winter and gives them courage. Many tigers were slaughtered and served in gourmet restaurants at the start of the Chinese Year of the Tiger in 1986. One businessman was able to save a beast from the butcher's knife. He bought the tiger for over $14,000 and it was released back into the wild. A group of Taiwan's Buddhist leaders bought a further twelve tigers that were being imported illegally from India and Bangladesh. But despite international control the trade in tiger products goes on.

Despite the ban on tiger products, they are still found for sale. Dealers claim their goods were acquired before the ban. This is often not true. Dealers say they can supply as many as 30 skins a month, knowing that animals will be killed illegally.

▷ There are many shops in Southeast Asia that sell tiger skins.

▽ All parts of the tiger are used. This tiger skull ashtray was spotted in a Bangkok shop window.

Habitat destruction

During the second half of the 20th century, a worldwide demand for hardwood has meant that the world's forests have been disappearing at a rate of 50 acres per minute. In 10 years, 40 percent of Malaysia's forests have been cut down. India has only 14 percent left and Bangladesh only 9 percent. The effect on the tiger, which is essentially a forest animal, has been catastrophic. Many tigers have found themselves with no place to live and no food to eat. Not only have the forests gone, but the prey animals that hide in them have gone too.

The decline in tiger numbers was one of the first signs that forest destruction has more widespread effects than just losing trees. Many plants and animals may disappear forever.

▽ These bulldozers are hauling logs out of the dwindling rain forest in Malaysia.

▽ This map shows that the living space of forest tigers is being rapidly lost.

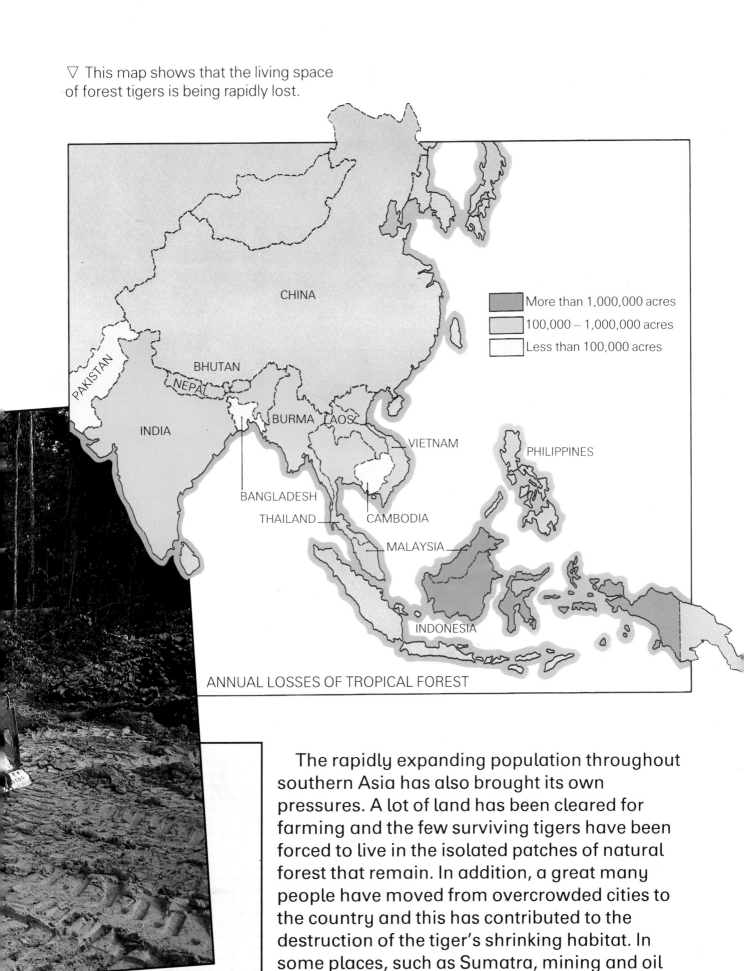

■ More than 1,000,000 acres	
■ 100,000 – 1,000,000 acres	
□ Less than 100,000 acres	

PAKISTAN
CHINA
BHUTAN
NEPAL
INDIA
BURMA LAOS
VIETNAM
PHILIPPINES
BANGLADESH
THAILAND
CAMBODIA
MALAYSIA
INDONESIA

ANNUAL LOSSES OF TROPICAL FOREST

The rapidly expanding population throughout southern Asia has also brought its own pressures. A lot of land has been cleared for farming and the few surviving tigers have been forced to live in the isolated patches of natural forest that remain. In addition, a great many people have moved from overcrowded cities to the country and this has contributed to the destruction of the tiger's shrinking habitat. In some places, such as Sumatra, mining and oil extraction have also disturbed forest areas.

Project tiger

On April 1, 1973, Indira Ghandi's Indian government launched Project Tiger. It was not just aimed at saving the tiger, but also at conserving the tiger's habitat. Reserves were established in the best tiger areas. People were kept out and whole villages were moved. Hunting was banned and the legal trade in tiger skins stopped. Anti-poaching patrols cracked down on poachers. Over $10 million of government money was allocated to staff and equip the reserves. The World Wildlife Fund (WWF) provided vehicles and equipment and the International Union for the Conservation of Nature and Natural Resources (IUCN) sent scientists to study the tigers there.

Several neighboring countries followed suit. Today Nepal, Bhutan, Bangladesh, Malaysia, Indonesia, Thailand, Korea, the Soviet Union and China have tiger protection programs. The results have exceeded expectations. Since Project Tiger started, tiger populations on reserves have more than doubled.

△ A tiger killed illegally in Sumatra.

▽ An anti-poaching patrol goes into action in Nepal's Royal Chitawan National Park.

Financial rewards for tiger poachers are high. With so much money at stake there are sometimes fierce battles between poachers and anti-poaching patrols. People on both sides have been killed. A tiger skin coat may have more than the blood of the tiger included in the price.

Reserves and research

At the same time as India was setting up its tiger reserves, neighboring Nepal also took action. The Nepalese government turned three of Nepal's finest hunting parks into tiger reserves. In one, the Royal Chitawan National Park, the Smithsonian Institute launched a long-term study of the wildlife. Tigers, leopards, bears and deer were all captured alive. The animals were then fitted with radio collars and released back into the reserve.

▷ The scientist in this photograph is fitting a radio transmitter collar to a tiger. The scientist can now follow it without getting too close. The everyday life of the tigers can be monitored without people disturbing the animals.

△ Tigers are tranquilized so that they can be studied.

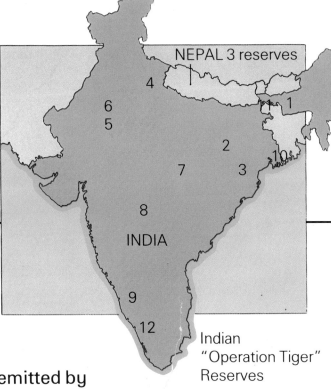

NEPAL 3 reserves

INDIA

Indian "Operation Tiger" Reserves

Scientists tracking the radio signals emitted by the transmitters followed the animals without disturbing their daily life. They discovered where the animals go and how they behave. This valuable information helped them to work out the best ways to manage the reserves and the animals living in them.

Today, the reserves are not just the homes of tigers and their accompanying scientists. They have also become tourist attractions where people can see tigers in the wild. Tourist parties ride on the backs of elephants into tiger territory.

1 Manas Reserve
2 Palamau National Park
3 Simlipal Reserve
4 Corbett National Park
5 Ranthambore Reserve
6 Sariska Reserve
7 Kanha Reserve
8 Melghat Reserve
9 Bandipur Reserve
10 Sundarbans Reserve
11 Jaldapara Reserve
12 Periyar Reserve

Man-eating tigers

Not everybody wants to save the tiger. In some parts of Asia tigers kill people. Humans are not usual tiger food, but old or sick animals which are unable to catch their normal prey may turn to man-eating. And it is perhaps not surprising that some people are killed – tiger populations are increasing, their habitats are shrinking, and people with no experience of wild animals are living near tiger territories.

One aspect of Project Tiger is to teach people how to live safely alongside wild tigers. But nevertheless serious outbreaks of man-eating still occur every year.

△ The armed guard above is patrolling an area containing known man-eaters. Attempts are made to put man-eaters in zoos.

▷ This Sunderbans woodcutter wears a mask on the back of his head. He hopes to fool any tiger that might try to stalk up behind him.

Sometimes tigers kill people after a chance encounter. Then, having discovered how easy it is to catch a human, they continue to hunt human prey. In some rural communities the man-eating tiger is a terrifying problem. In the Sunderbans Forest of Bangladesh, an average of 45 woodcutters, honey collectors and fishermen are killed by tigers each year. In the suburbs of Vladivostock in the Soviet Union, tigers have been seen waiting near bus stops for unwary prey. Where possible, man-eaters are tranquilized and moved elsewhere. If this is not possible, they are shot.

△ The man in this photograph is in fact an electrified wooden dummy. If a tiger attacks, it will get an electric shock. It may then leave humans alone.

△ Could captive tigers help save wild tigers in the future?

Tigers in zoos

In 1986, tiger experts from all over the world came together in Minnesota to agree on a Global Tiger Plan of Action. They were concerned that although numbers of tigers in the wild are increasing, the isolated populations will suffer from inbreeding. Inbreeding occurs when populations are so small that tigers breed with close relatives like brothers or sisters. This weakens the population. A small inbred population, for example, could be wiped out by an infectious disease. A normal, large population would be likely to contain individuals immune to the disease and it would survive.

One way to ensure a good mix of tigers is to breed them in captivity and then put them back into wild populations. Today, zoos all over the world are cooperating in trying to breed unrelated tigers. They hope that in the future, strong tiger stocks can be released into the remaining reserves to revitalize the surviving populations.

△ White tigers are often bred in zoos.

The tiger's future

Project Tiger has been very successful in a number of ways. The tiger itself survives and there are over 6,000 living in the wild today. Because of the reserves, large areas of land have been saved. This means that other wildlife can also survive in countries where land is valuable. And Project Tiger has encouraged governments (many from poorer nations) to work with conservation groups to save their natural heritage.

▽ This tiger illustrates the problem of lack of living space. She is running across farmland.

A painting of a tiger by the artist Rousseau was recently sold for one million dollars. It is sad that money for a painting of a tiger is so easy to obtain, yet money to save the tiger is so difficult.

◁ This tiger cub was born in Mexico Zoo. It will live. The Balinese tiger in the picture is now extinct.

Project Tiger has also helped change attitudes. Farmers have realized, for instance, that tigers are not always dangerous pests but can actually help to control the pests on their land. Wild pigs thrive and damage crops in areas where tigers have been removed. The management of water resources on tiger reserves has helped neighboring villages – many now have water instead of dry streams.

The importance of tiger conservation can be summed up in a speech made by Indira Ghandi when Project Tiger began. "The tiger's future," she said, "is our future."

The largest tiger is the male Siberian tiger. It can be up to 13ft long and weigh 850lb. Males of the most common tiger, the Indian, can be 8-10ft long, stand 30in at the shoulder and weigh 330-550lb. Male Javan and Sumatran tigers grow to 9ft and weigh 330lb. The females of all types are slightly smaller.

Tiger markings

In a zoo, the stark orangy-yellow, black and white colors of the tiger's fur stand out clearly from the background. In the tiger's natural habitat, in the forest or in tall grass where brightly sunlit patches alternate with long, dark shadows, the stripes break up the animal's outline and make it almost invisible. This effective camouflage allows the tiger to get close to its prey without being seen.

Researchers are able to identify individual tigers by the pattern of markings above the eyes. Each is different. The eight subspecies are different too. The northern races, like the Siberian tiger, tend to have longer and thicker fur than the tropical ones.

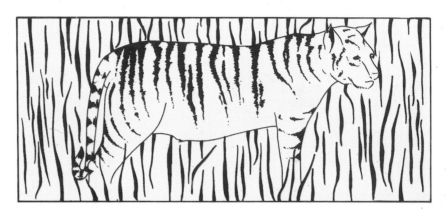

The tiger's range

Male and female tigers have home ranges that do not overlap with others of the same sex. But a male tiger's range may overlap with many females' ranges.

Female Indian tigers have 8 sq miles of home range, while males have 25-40 sq miles. Siberian tigers have larger home ranges because their prey are spread out.

Home ranges are marked by urine mixed with secretions from an anal gland. This is sprayed on trees, bushes and rocks. It tells other tigers to keep out.

Daily life

Tigers are mainly solitary animals, although they do come together at certain times. The basic family unit is a mother and her cubs, but groups of males and females have been seen together in the wild. Tigers spend many hours visiting all parts of their home range. Neighbors will take over any ground that has not been scent marked within three to four weeks. All tigers need to survive is food, water and somewhere to hide, whether it be in the snow or in the tropics.

Tiger fact file 2

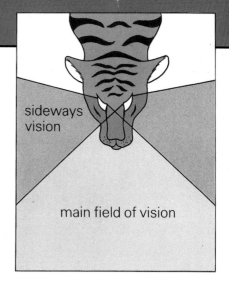

sideways vision

main field of vision

Hunting

Tigers hunt mainly alone. Individuals might travel 12 miles during the night in search of suitable prey. Even then, they are not always successful. It may take up to 20 tries before catching a meal.

Tigers like to eat medium-sized herbivores, such as sambar, chital and swamp deer, red and rusa deer, and wild pigs. Occasionally tigers eat large animals such as gaur and rhino. Recently a research scientist even witnessed two tigers bringing down an elephant, although this is unusual. Below, a tiger is catching a monkey.

A hunting tiger first locates its prey by smell and then closes in slowly using sight. It stalks downwind, hidden from view by vegetation. It relies on stealth and its camouflaged coat to approach within 65 ft before giving chase. It does not leap onto its prey, but after a short run attacks from the side or the rear. It will slap the hind legs or the rump to slow the prey down. Having caught up, it seizes the victim's neck or shoulder in its mouth. The tiger's hind feet remain on the ground and the prey is jerked off balance. The prey is suffocated with a bite to the throat.

Vision

Like many hunting animals, the tiger has binocular vision. This enables the animal to judge distances accurately. It also has good side vision. Most tigers have yellowish eyes, but white tigers have blue eyes.

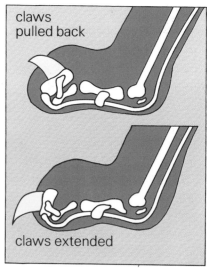

claws pulled back

claws extended

Claws

In common with other cats, the tiger has claws which can be pulled back or exposed when catching prey.

Feeding

A tiger feels uncomfortable in the open. Consequently it will drag the prey it has killed into the undergrowth or to the water before beginning to feed. It usually starts on the rump. A large carcass can last for two or three days. Each night 44-77 lb of meat will be consumed. An adult tiger needs about 15-20 lb of meat daily to survive – a total of three tonnes per year. This is the equivalent of 30 domestic cattle or 70 axis deer each year. A solitary tigress will kill every eight days, whereas a female with cubs needs more food and will try to kill every five to six days.

In legends it says that tigers imitate the contact calls of their prey animals to attract them within striking distance. This is probably not true. Tigers grunt when surprised. They have a variety of calls. The loudest is the roar which is given after a kill. It says to other tigers "stay away." When large food items are scarce, a tiger turns to smaller prey. It will snap up salmon from a river, take frogs and small rodents, and may even eat birds' eggs and berries. It does not always kill its own food. It would not hesitate to rob a leopard of its kill.

If it is disturbed during its meal, a tiger will give a warning growl. If the annoyance persists, it opens its mouth, pulls back its lips, flattens its ears, narrows its eyes, and snarls. The tail twitches from side to side and the tiger begins to hiss and spit. Eventually, it will attack.

Teeth

The tiger's muscular jaws give a powerful shearing bite. Its long canines help to kill prey. Sharp cheek teeth tear at the meat.

Tiger fact file 3

Courtship and mating

When a male tiger enters a female's home range, he will check her scent markings for signs that she is ready to mate. Mating can take place at any time of the year in tropical areas, but only in the winter months in the north. Females are receptive for only a few days. Tigers at mating time are noisy with moans and subdued roars. When two tigers approach one another they puff and make snorting sounds.

When a female tiger is ready to accept a male, she snorts and touches his whiskers with her own. She rolls on the ground and lies on her back. The male stands over her, emits a series of cough-like roars, and seizes her by the neck. They then mate. When mating is over, the female jumps up, throwing the male off her. During the course of a few days to a week, this can occur up to a hundred times.

Tigers are ready to breed at three to four years of age. The gestation period is from 95-112 days. Litters in the wild are usually three to four cubs, although the Indian tigress "Baghdad" at a zoo in Redwood City gave birth to eight cubs in 1972. Cubs are about 33cm (13 in) long at birth and weigh about 1kg (2.2 lb).

The young

The cubs are raised by the female alone. They are born blind and helpless in a "den." The eyes open after ten days. Baby teeth develop in the second week. The cubs have stripes but their colors are lighter than the parents. They darken after four months. They drink milk for six months but begin to eat small quantities of meat after two months. The mother may leave them in the early days to go hunting. The cubs are dependent on their mother for food and protection until they are 18 months old.

Growing up

The independent cubs are tolerated in their mother's home range until they are 2-2½ years old. After this time they are chased away. They must move to another area and carve out a home range of their own. Groups of young adults are often found on the outskirts of established home ranges. They wait to take over a range that has become vacant through the death of a tiger, or they barge in between two home ranges — perhaps where a female with cubs cannot visit all her range.

Index

A Afghanistan 7
anti-poaching patrols 16, 17

B Balinese tiger 7, 9, 25
Bangkok 12
Bangladesh 12, 14, 16, 21

C camouflage 26
captive breeding 23
Caspian tiger 7
China 7, 11, 16
claws 28

D daily life 27
dealers 12
deer 18
disease 23

E extinction 4, 7, 9

F farming 4, 11, 15, 25
feeding 14, 28, 29
financial rewards 12, 17
forest destruction 14-15, 20, 24
fur coats 4, 12, 17

G Ghandi, Indira 16, 25
Global Tiger Plan of Action 23
growing up 31

H habitat 4, 7-9, 14-16, 20
height 26
home ranges 27, 31
Hong Kong 12
hunting 4, 8-9, 11, 16

I inbreeding 23
India 7, 8-9, 11, 12, 14, 16, 18
Indian (Bengal) tiger 7, 26, 27
Indochinese (Corbett's) tiger 7
Indonesia 16
International Union for the Conservation of Nature and Natural Resources (IUCN) 16
Iran 7

J Japan 12
Javan tiger 7, 26

K Korea 7, 16

L law 11, 26
leopards 18
litters 30

M Maharajahs 8, 9
Malaysia 14, 16
man-eating tigers 20-21
markings 26
mating 30
meat 11, 12
Mexico Zoo 25

N Nepal 11, 16, 17, 18

P pest control 25
poaching 11, 12, 17
poisoning 11
prey 14, 20, 26, 28
Project Tiger 4, 16, 20, 24, 25

R radio tracking 18
research 18
reserves 16, 18, 24, 25
Royal Chitawan National Park 17, 18

S Siberia 7
Siberian (Manchurian) tiger 7, 26, 27
Singapore 12
skins 4, 12, 16
Smithsonian Institute 18
South Chinese tiger 7
Southeast Asia 7, 12
Soviet Union 16, 21
sport 4, 8-9
Sumatra 11, 15, 16
Sumatran tiger 7, 26
Sunderbans Forest 20, 21

T Taiwan 12
teeth 29
Thailand 16
tourism 18
trade in tigers 4, 12, 16
traps 11

U United States 18, 23

V vision 28
Vladivostok 21

W water resources 25
weight 26
white tigers 23, 28
wild pigs 25
World Wildlife Fund (WWF) 16

Photographic Credits:
Cover and pages 4-5, 14, 23, 27 (top), 29 and 30: Planet Earth; pages 8-9, 10, 13 and 16: World Wildlife Fund International; pages 11, 12, 17, 19, 21 and 25: Bruce Coleman; pages 18, 26 and 28: Survival Anglia; pages 20 and 20-21: Magnum; pages 22 and 31 (top): Frank Lane Agency; page 24: World Wildlife Fund UK; page 27 (bottom): Ardea; page 31 (bottom): NHPA.

PRINTED IN BELGIUM BY
proost
INTERNATIONAL BOOK PRODUCTION